The Daughter of the King

Dorothy Cusick

En Route Books and Media, LLC
St. Louis, MO

⊕ENROUTE
Make the time

En Route Books and Media, LLC
5705 Rhodes Avenue
St. Louis, MO 63109

Cover credit: Dorothy Cusick
with calligraphy by Carol Savage

Copyright © 2023 Dorothy Cusick

ISBN-13: 979-8-88870-096-9
Library of Congress Control Number: 2022949255

No part of this book may be reproduced, stored in a retrieval system, or transmitted in any form, or by any means, electronic, mechanical, photocopying, or otherwise, without the prior written permission of the author.

To my sister, Marilyn,
who lives in my heart.

Foreword

This brief but moving tribute is written by Dorothy Cusick about the faith journey of her mother Mary, "The Daughter of the King." With a mystic mind and heart, Dorothy probes deeply into the life of her poverty-stricken mother. As one of eight children evicted from their home, Dorothy rode with her mother on the streetcar back and forth as they searched for a place for their family.

Mary's only hope was in God. She found relatives to take in the sons and was given temporary housing for herself and her two daughters with the Salvation Army. When she went to her pastor, he suggested that she find an orphanage to take in her children. She found this totally unacceptable. Later, he found her a temporary apartment.

Homelessness drove Mary to God in prayer. There, she found hope to drive herself forward. She found a job that helped her get an apartment and begin to pay off bills. She prayed her way through each day.

I think that this is a very inspirational book for all who are crushed by poverty, by broken relationships, and by life's circumstances. It is riddled with powerful scriptures that again and again demonstrate that the "Lord hears the cry of the poor." The very poverty that literally crushed Mary drove her to become "The Daughter of the King."

I hope that this short inspirational book finds its way into the hands of those who are crushed in spirit because of physical poverty. The deep faith of Mary Cusick is catching!

> Most Rev. Robert J. Hermann
> Bishop Emeritus
> Archdiocese of St. Louis

A Tribute to our Mother, Mary Cusick

She gave Him her rag-tag heart, tattered and worn,
To mend the broken pieces, shattered and torn.

He returned it to her shiny, made new,
Bearing the imprint of His image, love born anew.

Love freely given,
She freely gave back to the ones He sent her way.

To our mother, Mary, with heart so true,
And to the One who made it new,
All our thanksgiving, honor and praise to you.

Thank you to:

Bishop Robert Hermann for your open heart that was able to discern the story hidden within;

My brother, Tim, for your unfailing encouragement and critique of the artwork;

My brother, Tom, for your continued interest;

Karen Price for your exceptional editing skills and transforming pen to type;

Carol Savage, the calligrapher, for your beautiful dancing letters.

Whoever loves me will keep my word, and my father will love him and we will come to him and make our dwelling with him.

John 14:23

Chapter 1

Nibble after crunchy nibble of winter's bitter, biting cold, and fallen, fallen went the anguished cry throughout the unadorned, shriveled-up land. Stripped of its majestic grandeur, its barrenness an affront to its former glory days, languishing in a state of inertia, its scraggly stick-like figures awaited the Master's life-giving touch.

Stirred by His blustery sigh, the balmy southern winds blew their beguiling breeze, wreathing the chilled exposed trees in soothing whispers of "be not afraid." Surrender, like a lover, to the warm caress of His wake-up kiss. Squeezed by His strong right hand, spongy moisture-laden clouds drizzled down, their wetness burrowing the ground. Drip after delicate drip-drop of playful raindrops trickling down to the underground beat out their splish-splash refrain: "He makes all things new again," as they tickled to life dormant treasures buried below, sleeping through winter's cold. Beckoned by His darting, dancing sunbeams tapping out the way, burgeoning seedlings, pregnant with life, wriggle through the muck and mire, fretting out their passageways into His light of day.

And like a puppeteer, who enlivened his wiry, wobbly puppets by a pull on their strings, with the gentle nudge of His unstrung hands, the Master drew his lush extravaganza to life. Rising up from beds below, mounting their thrones as if kings and queens royally-robed, sat Earth's flowering profusion of unveiled colors enthroned. Smiling, He proclaimed, "Fait Accompli! Adieu Winter! Hello Spring!"

Dusty millers, shake off your dirt! Ready yourselves for the "Praise Parade." Royal-robed violas, strum a gladsome tune! Persnickety Virginia bluebells, chime in too! Bleeding Hearts, splash a dab of color to brighten the drab! Climb to the heavens, Jacob's ladder! Glimpse your Creator and tease an admiring glance.

Arrange your rows, coquettish daffodils! Sway to and fro in the gentle breeze, commencing your annual dance of praise as you bow before the Lord.

All you flowery show-offs, arrayed in delicate splendor, accord a fitting accolade! Bless the Lord!

It was into this milieu of Spring's fanciful spray of delights that Mary, so fearfully and so wonderfully made, commanded the starring role in her 1910 May debut. As father Johnny and mother Mame cradled innocence in their arms, drawn were they into a mysterious awareness, imperceptible, yet palpable, of participating in a happening divine.

For be attentive, you who have eyes to see and ears to hear. Rouse yourselves. Raise your sights. Look beyond and entertain the thought that there was more to this tranquil, serene scene, not caught with the natural eye. Still yourself. Draw near. See the fluttering wings! Hear the mellifluous canticles of joy! For on that day, in that very room, a celestial gathering of angels convened, commanded to guard the daughter of the King in all her ways.

Father Johnny plied his carpentry trade, while mother Mame, fruitful, gave birth to five more frilly-dressed little girls and two rough-and-tumble little boys.

Now, eight rambunctious children buzzing about like busy bees in an incredibly shrinking house too small for their needs, presented a dilemma. What was Johnny to do?

Confident that even the dreams of a poor, lowly man could become reality, Johnny stretched out his hand, like the Biblical man with the withered hand.

Wielding his hammer like a magician wields a wand – abracadabra – before his eyes it stood, regal and tall, eliciting oohs and aahs and envious sighs from passersby, the roomier house Johnny built for the family he loved.

Lacy Irish curtains in the windows, knickknacks in every nook and cranny, made the house uniquely their own. But the table of plenty Mame set before them, where each drank from the cup of human kindness and feasted on meals prepared with a pinch of patience, a dash of understanding, a sprinkle of forgiveness and a sweet dollop of love, made it a home.

In this home where love abounded, Mary grew by leaps and bounds, savoring sips of royal favors, poured forth from His cup of sweet inexplicable mysteries, of which she did partake. When was it they first met, this One her heart could not forget, who opened heaven's treasures to her, and setting His seal upon her heart, pledged His everlasting love?

He, as first mover, turned Mary's mind to thoughts of Him. Gradually, He revealed to her heart, truths her mind could not conceive. He awakened her heart with the warmth of His love, igniting longings for Him. As she said "yes," He came to live in that place meant only for Him. There was a place deep in Mary's heart where only He could go. Nothing or no one could enter there. It was made for Him alone. And like the little halcyon bird that built its nest into a ball, she nestled in His heart, all wrapped up in Him, but alas, life's fragility wormed its way in.

It was springtime. All was blissfully sunny and fine, for a time.

Chapter 1

Wide-eyed Mary and little sister, Dorothy, ogled the fragrant, delicate masterpieces upon their creeping vines, as up the arched latticework, lackadaisically they climbed. To the top, they inched their carpet of new dawn roses, unrolling it along the way like a flamboyant colorful display, cascading over the two below, lost in happy-go-lucky play.

Frolicking in the enchanted rose garden, passing the day so merry and gay, a dreadful foreboding surfacing from the cavernous depths below, froze the two in play with its shrill, ear-piercing cry, "nevermore," shattering the joy of the day.

Naivete's innocence locked eyes with terror's guile which held the key, unlocking the pit, unleashing death, the never-invited guest who plucked Dorothy's blush of life away.

It was summertime. All was amusingly funny and fine, for a time.

Loquacious brother, Jackie, cute and curly-headed only five, was a curious little guy, always inquiring about his bony shoulder blades, for he had surmised they must be wings to carry him to heaven on high. The scoundrel of destruction, however, had a less lofty setting in mind for Jackie to spend his time.

Underhandedly, eyes darting to-and-fro, cautiously drawing the pall over his grotesquely-repulsive state, the scoundrel anxiously lay in wait. A speeding car, screeching tires, a blood-curdling scream and the boy's little body lay lifeless in the street. With an unquenchable thirst that drooled with delight, the master of deception, who drank in death like sweet nectar from the gods, readied himself to swallow up Jackie, but he had wings like a dove, and up and away he flew into his heavenly home.

Yes, into Mary's footloose and fancy-free life walked tragedy's dismay, sharing its cup foaming over with a bitter, bubbly brew of misery and pain. Out walked a downcast, heavy-hearted girl, leaving the carefree, little girl behind.

Set me as a seal on your heart, as a seal on your arm.

Song of Songs 8:6b

Chapter 2

It was a time to grow, to embrace and to be far from embraces, a time to leave behind that which was known, a time to face the unknown. It was a time to slip into the ever-enlarging territory of young adult life and to try it on for size.

Onto the path of life stepped Mary, one foot forward in heightened expectation, one foot back with trepidation nipping at her heel. With eyes feasting on the world's endless possibilities, but with a heart hungry for more, on tiptoes to the heavens she reached for the elusive stars whose alluring magnetism pulled all of her sought-after wishes from down below up to them. Stunningly, snip, snip, as if cut-outs from the dark backdrop of night, her wished-upon stars tumbled head over heels, like a clumsy lover, into her star-struck heart.

Amused, she reflected. Hoped-for wishes must weave their intangible threads throughout the fabric of everyday life. Or why had God created the stars and the heights if they were not meant to be reached for and realized? With a twinkle in her eyes, walking the firm foundation laid by Johnny and Mame, to the train station she went and boarded the eastbound train for New York City and the ride of her life.

In this bustling city bigger than life, amid the cacophonous dissonant sounds and glaring neon lights, the night air, animated and electrified by love, sizzled with heightened expectation at Mary and Pat's first embrace.

A tall, lanky handsome prince was he, with a stellar reputation as the "best catch" on Scranton's south side, and quite the charmer, everyone agreed. Smitten was she, taken captive by those light blue, starry eyes that stirred up fire in her soul with their penetrating, amorous gaze. Surrender to this all-consuming fire of love, her soul adjured. Let its sparks rise like flickering fireflies to kiss love's summit, the heavenly flame. Cleave to Pat in that covenant bond where two flames form one fire of love. She obliged.

Choosing from a kaleidoscope of vibrant colors reflecting love's passions to be, painstakingly, Mary set

Chapter 2

about to paint on her wedding-day canvas, a facsimile of the new life meant to be. Every brilliant hue so dazzlingly bright, eclipsed only by each intricate brushstroke, captured a magical life scene imaging every mused – about hope and dream.

Could any landscape of painted love stir the heart like this Claude Lorrain masterpiece? Certainly not, quipped she, unaware of the subtle undetected imperfections in the canvas itself.

A cordial welcome, extended to the wedding guests passing through the church doors, returned beaming smiles and sunny eyes in kind. Guests engaged in chit-chat, serving up family stories like warm slices of bread, jostled for the choicest seats, while guests with eyes eager for the razzle-dazzle of frivolity, surveyed the wedding scene, surprised by its solemnity. The unseen, peppered with excitement, amplified the already-charged atmosphere, abruptly silenced by the organ's sonorous commencement of the Wedding March.

Blithesomely buoyant, as if walking on marshmallow feet, Mary, the Irish bride-to-be, sprang lightly down the aisle in a homemade gown, fashioned lovingly by Mame, created from a soft, gossamer-like fabric and fine Irish lace, so delicate, it looked as though snow-flakes alighted there, only to stay. Why even the elegant, stately roses, with their proclivity for flare, unable to match love's sweet radiant beauty, blushed and bowed as she passed by. With promises of undying love, sealed by the hand of God in a covenant bond, graces "in good measure, packed together, shaken down and overflowing," poured out over them.

Effervescence bubbled from the spirited bride like

confetti being tossed in the air. Zestfully, she gushed, "Lolla-palooza, how glorious it is to luxuriate in the joy of the day!" But underneath a veneer of civility, like storm clouds set to darken a sunny day, disingenuous remarks concerning her modest dress boiling up from the scalding cauldron of steamy wedding day gossip, extinguished any notion of seeing herself as a lacy Irish bride. Until the lover who sought her beauty, caught her eye.

Then, off went the two to dance the dance to the rhythm of new life as freely they drank from love's sweet wedding cup, inextricably united in love's repose, body to body, mind to mind and soul to soul.

Gift after gift from heaven they came, formed and knitted in Mary's womb. With utmost tenderness, each precious infant, welcomed with wonderment like the babe in Simeon's arms, was tucked into the quiver with care. One graceful fair-haired girl with ringlets of reddish-gold, was swaddled snuggly in a bunting of pink.

Warmly cocooned in buntings of blue were boy, after boy, after boy, after boy, after cherub-faced boy. Oh, but on a day in May, with exuberance unrestrained, a lilting, lyrical refrain, not to be contained, burst forth as Mary excitedly sang: "I got a girl! I got a girl!" Swathed in a mother's loving embrace, gingerly into the quiver, the last little girl went, leaving room for one more, another bouncing baby boy.

There were eight babies in all to grow a mother's soul. From on high, God pronounced a blessing on the fruit of her womb. And as each infant was baptized, they were born again – but from above into His divine family – God's family of love.

In the shadow of your wings I take refuge till the storms of destruction pass by.

Psalm 57:26

Chapter 3

Under the cover of night, in the guise of a non-threatening sky, lurked the evil eye of the storm, furtively scanning the horizon for its death-dealing forces, the savagely wild winds of change. Unite. Mount up, mighty winds of mayhem. Loose yourselves. Unleash your chaos. Rail mercilessly against Mary and her family!

They roared. They pounded. They pummeled. They laid waste, sweeping away all that was known into a whirl-wind of confusion, leaving them lost and alone. He that "weighed out the winds," rebuked them and their destructive force. But the winds that brought the Spirit, which breathed new life into dry men's bones, He did not restrain, but called upon them to bring to this family His life-giving grace.

A rather lovely, spacious upstairs flat in south St. Louis was the family's residence when, on that infamous September day in 1946, misfortune came knocking on the door, demanding they pack their bags and be on their way. An imposing figure was he, the uniformed man with ice in his veins, who clinked and clanked, as he entered the room. His unfamiliar face, transparent with lingering gloom, signaled this was not an innocuous visit, but one of doom. Two words – bold and syrupy black – oozed from his relinquished devastating document, like slippery slime, gobbling up Mary's inner light.

On that bleak September day, her countenance took on the persona of a Mother of Sorrows. As the depth of love for her family magnified the sorrow she felt, all thoughts held captive surrendered to anguish so great, a heart broken and shattered, cried out to heaven for help and for grace.

Furniture and belongings so carefully maintained, now dismantled and pitched every which way, went out of the flat and to the curb they came, discarded as useless rubbish, awaiting trash pickup the next day. Like little troopers, the seven petrified children marched to folly's dastardly unfamiliar tune, as the sheriff shooed them out, locking the door to the deafening silence of the vacant flat and the crumpled "Eviction Notice" tossed on the floor.

"He found them in the wilderness, a wasteland of howling desert. He shielded them and cared for them, guarding them as the apple of His eye." Spreading His wings to receive them, "He bore them up on His pinions," placing them in the outstretched arms of the Schneider family who tendered to them a short reprieve from the vicissitudes of life until winter's unrelenting, precarious plight.

St. Louis Globe-Democrat.

NOW THEY HAVE 12 CHILDREN

MODEL CHILDREN was the tag put on the offspring of Mr. and Mrs. Patrick Cusick by Mrs. N. A. Schneider, 2931 Utah st., after she had taken the family into her home following its eviction from quarters at 3400 Utah. Five children live with Mr. and Mrs. Cusick at the Schneider home, while two others have gone to the home of an aunt in Fort Smith, Ark. Dr. and Mrs. Schneider have five children of their own in the 10-room house. Shown in the Schneider home, from the left, are: Timothy Cusick, 6; Marilyn, 14, holding Dorothy, 14 months; Michael, 4; Mrs. Cusick, and Tommy, 2½. —Globe-Democrat Photo

This is my commandment: Love one another as I love you. No one has greater love than this, to lay down one's life for one's friends.

John 15:12-13

Chapter 4

Dotting the winter landscape, perfuming the air with their fresh scent of pine, evergreens laden with Christmas lights hazily aglow through a dusting of freshly-fallen snow, spread their branches as if to shelter the crèche below. Storefront windows, decorated with garland and tinseled trees, paraded their latest finery of gifts and toys as last-minute shoppers scurrying about like hurried little mice, finished their hustle and bustle from store to store. Toting shopping bags stuffed to overflowing with presents galore, scrambling to board the Grand Avenue streetcar, they headed for home.

Inquisitive eyes gave a cursory look, but seeing only a heap of clothes on the seat at the back of the streetcar, quickly glanced away. Wearing the poor man's garb of invisibility, a mother and her two girls huddled together on the seat at the back of the streetcar went completely unnoticed by those who had eyes but could not see.

From morning light into darkness of night, up and down the avenue they rode, heading to a destination unknown for they had no place to call home. That night, the darkest of nights, a light shone through the darkness, illuminating a sign, transforming a mother's face strained with care, from a blank, expressionless stare into a hopeful, expectant gaze.

On that biting, cold Christmas Eve of 1946, off the streetcar the three stepped, into the open arms of hospitality's warm embrace. Accompany them inside. See they are only three of the many forgotten souls, wayfarers in the night, cordially welcomed by the Salvation

Army and given a meal, a bed and a genuine smile.

Envision the disparity when visiting quaint memories from Mary's past. See the joyful gathering of family in Scranton, all eyes mesmerized by Johnny's winter wonderland created around the perfect Christmas tree.

Now, notice the three as they kneel before their only Christmas treasure – a miniature Nativity scene. With rosary beads clutched tightly in her hands, Mary seems lost in prayer.

Surely on Christmas Eve, angels took her prayers to the altar of gold, along with the incense from countless Masses that arose to the Lord, for during fitful sleep, an answer to her heart's cries came in three little words.

"Come to me," they seemed to say, the outstretched arms of the Infant King born in a stable in Bethlehem. "Come to me," echoed the same refrain from the outstretched arms of the Humble King on the rugged cross at Calvary.

She came to Him, empty of hope, desolate of consolation. She came to Him, disquieted by events and tormented with pain. She came to Him to touch His heart. She came to Him on bended knees.

Before the crucifix, like a voice heard in Ramah, Rachel, lamenting the children who were no more, Mary's cup overflowing with sorrow, poured out with a plaintiff cry bewailing her five sons with relatives and so far away. Was there hope of uniting their family once more?

Hauntingly drawn, as if seized by an inescapable hold, she surveyed the face of the One lifted up on the cross, marveling how, though motionless and uttering not a word, it held the power to move an anxious heart to quietude with the symphony of love scored on every line of its painfully notable face. Oh, twisted distorted face! Who could not avow the story of unfathomable love told in the midst of such travail? Who could not vouchsafe love's final utterance, expressed not in words, but to the very depth of a soul's sigh after loving sigh?

> "Come, all you who pass by the way. Look and see whether there is any suffering like my suffering, which has been dealt me."
> – Lamentation 1:12

He was the suffering servant, the light who walked into a dark, formidable garden, his face diffused with sorrow so great, agony hung from every tree as if conjoined to his suffering. He was the one pondering a grave decision, who answered it in drop after drop of his precious blood. His was the hideously marred, crucified body from whom men looked askance, repulsed by his scourging, worn like a wine presser's scarlet gown. His was the pierced heart, opened like a door never to be shut, from which flowed the triumph of the cross, a sweet, fragrant oblation to the Father of no greater love.

That was the day the sun retreated, hiding its face, the day rivers gulped a sigh and Creation's cry pierced heaven, as it rumbled and quaked, unsettled and furiously enraged at witnessing His ignominious, vile death. That was the day a silence of awe blanketed an earth which was hushed and bowed down in reverence to this Holy One. That was the day death scoffed at life, thinking it had the final say.

But could death's blow slay the plans of the Author of Life? Or could death's dark tendrils hold bound the

Son's rising light? Enter through the garden's gate. Stand before His tomb. He is not there. Only the sting of death and the shame of the cross are entombed there. Glory and majestic power, once concealed and now revealed, burst forth from that dark, dank tomb, shining its refulgent light on creation made new again, ushered in on the new eighth day when Christ, the vanquisher of sin and death, reconciled mankind to the Father.

Now, beneath the sweetheart tree, warmed by the candle's glow, Mary stared down at her crossroad. She came to touch His heart, but it was her heart that was touched when she looked His way. Her very suffering became a shared participation in His suffering on the cross. Her wounds were His wounds. His wounds were her wounds. And the wounds that drew now became the chains that forever bound the two together in the affections of the heart.

The only response worthy of love's extravagant nobility, made visible by Christ on the cross, was that same selfless outpouring of love. Not calculating the cost, taking up her cross, she stepped out in faith, assured that on that final day, when it was laid at Christ's feet, intimated in her cross was His victory.

We are making our way toward the light of our heavenly home with the grace of Christ leading us and showing us the way. The light of his grace was also symbolized by the cloud and the pillar of fire which protected the Israelites from darkness throughout their journey and brought them by a wonderful path to their promised homeland.

Saint Bede

Chapter 5

Starved for direction, seeking to squeeze a little possibility out of impossibility, to bind together rather than to rend apart, what advice had Mary expected to hear from Father Cornelius Flavin at the rectory that day? Not this dirge, this requiem to her family, reverberating like a gong ringing in her ears as his jolting words, not wanted to be heard but needed to be said, rolled effortlessly off his tongue, like tumbleweed being carried about at the whim of the wind. "Mary, you have to put your children in the orphanage."

Was this the wise counsel of a Solomon? You will see.

A washed-out wasteland of white secreted Father Flavin away, as images of her seven forlorn, freckled-face children, as dear to her as David to Jonathan, flashed one by one before her eyes, engendering a boundless love in a mother's pain-riddled heart. Thus it began – the struggle within.

Down the corridor, in and out of the convoluted maze of the labyrinth to the very depth of her soul, terrified expectant hope took flight, seeking refuge from the gauntlet of hounding despair, doggedly on its tail. To no avail, hounding despair, like the blood-thirsty savagery of a wolfish beast, barking its endless, repetitious harassing words, "put your children in the orphanage," tore and slashed expectant hope into bits and pieces, spewing it down toward the pit of hell.

But from the rotten, sinking, maggoty cesspool of the

lake of conflagration, fumed the angry, searing rebuke: "Turn back, hope! Turn back, you harbinger of brighter days! Only dispirited despair may enter this dreaded, despicable, dark prison of the never-ending hell."

As shades of indigo blue washed away in the bright golden nuance of a hopeful new day, eyes that could not see beyond to a future without her seven children, opened. Choosing love over fear, unflinchingly Mary's pronouncement came. "My children will never be put in an orphanage."

Out of the dry, parched, barren desert, through the stormy clouds of day and the fiery trials of night, He led them to the highway called the holy way, where, with joy and gladness they met, the lost family of nine. Weary and bedraggled, into the humble two-bedroom home, found by Father Flavin, they came. Strained and cramped in quarters so tight, they pulled and tugged, pushed and shoved, stretching the creaking groaning walls to gain an inch or two for soon another baby would be born, rounding out the family count to ten. Yes, a house they had, made of mortar and stone; but within they had much more – a mother who, when queried, chose the royal road.

Standing beside the pathways of old, she inquired of them the way to go. It was opened up to her as they answered back: "Choose the blessing. Choose goodness. Choose life." Further, she asked how to keep her feet firmly planted on the royal road. They replied: "Do what is right and follow the Holy One who bears the imprints of the crucifixion on His hands, feet and side."

For many fall prey to Lady Folly, who strings them along with her cheap imitation pearls at no price. Spun from the sticky snare of her spurious web, and strung together with alluring machinations couched in love and care, they become prisoners entangled there. Others, dazed by her chicanery and duplicitous schemes, seeing not the carnage, tread instead the valley of decision, where languish the living dead, reeling and recoiling at the litany of woes pronounced there.

Now, on this perilous journey, how could Mary see the path to take if not for His Word, like a lamp to light the way? How could she keep from stumbling except for His strong right hand to uphold and guard her coming and going along the way?

May the Lord reward what you have done! May you receive a full reward from the Lord, the God of Israel, under whose wings you have come for refuge.

Ruth 2:12

Chapter 6

Life's difficulties, fraught with ambiguity, abound. That "I do," promised long ago, encompassed more than Mary ever imagined, as pictures of present-day experiences bore little resemblance to those breathtaking images painted on her wedding-day canvas.

He came one day to a wedding feast in Cana of Galilee and left behind a miraculous portrait for all mankind to see. As the Master Painter of scenes, He was inclined to view them a bit differently. Recall the widow with the meager offering of two small coins. The poorest of the poor, He saw as the richest of all. When plumbing the depths of the blind man's fixed, expressionless eyes, His all-knowing eyes saw what the Pharisees could not – that Bartimaeus, son of Timaeus, saw with the eyes of faith. With a venomous, victorious hiss of disdain, evil gloated at Christ on the cross, until slithering upon the resurrection scene, he heard trumpeted the words, "Reprobate, condemned you are forever and a day."

Yielding up her store-bought wedding-day canvas, washed out by the grime of daily living and harsh, intense realities of life, it was freely given up to the only One with a heavenly canvas on which to paint life's consummate masterpiece.

Impish bedfellows from that eviction past toyed with her mind, unsettling her sleep. Seeking deliverance from those vexing tyrants of the mind – would have, could have and should have – which clung like heavy armor, weighing her down; she parlayed an exchange as she knelt before her King.

Off came the shackles that bound, as He put on His lightweight armor of power and strength. Now, tripping the light fantastic to the same replayed ditty became her new forte, day after grinding day: "Ho hum, beat the drum. Rise and shine, be to work by nine. Return home by ten, collapse in the bed, for soon it would be time to rise and shine and begin again."

Week after week, month after month, year after year, clickity-clack, clickity-clack, up the hill to work went mother Mary in her high-heeled shoes. Then, clickity-clack, clickity-clack, down the hill back home she came, wearing out shoe after shoe, but never her resolve.

Corners are meant to be turned, and thus were Mary's. Quickening their steps, the high heels conveyed the purveyor of good news, home at an accelerated pace. With deed in hand, verifying ownership of the little rented house, all the riffraff – those clinging pesky rascals from that eviction past – were packed up and booted right out of the little house, at the end of the street, which stood in the shadow cast by a sacrificial hill.

The hill that was too steep to climb at times, paradoxically, could be mounted on bended knees. It was a hill where weighty encumbrances were lightened by divesting of self, a hill where desires of the heart were not plucked from the heights, but gathered from the depths of its hallowed ground. It was a hill where echoes of Mary's petitions could stair-step the stars to the heavens, as humbly she knelt in prayer.

Remind me, Lord, when I am old and gray, of Your pledged fidelity.
Remind me, Lord, when my strength is gone and I fear

Chapter 6

*the dark shadows
before the dawn, that they take flight, bathed in Your
radiant light.
Remind me, Lord, when all seems lost, that I found my
delight
and joy in You alone.*

Happy the man
who finds wisdom,
the man who gains
understanding!...
Her ways are pleasant
ways, and all her paths
are peace; She is a
tree of life to those
who grasp her and
he is happy who
holds her fast.

Proverbs 3:13, 17-18

Chapter 7

Before the beaming chubby-faced sun cast an inquisitive peek over the horizon, or the new day unrolled its story like a scroll, in the shadows of bygone yesterdays, a menagerie of unforgettable ornamental keepsakes dangled in disarray from each child's personalized memory tree. Flashing back to superfluous notions, each braggadocios bauble spun a yarn a mile long, or snagged a fish with many tales, cluttering the mind with a hodgepodge of inconsequential memories.

Now, separate and distinct from the pretentious, personalized memory tree was the one known as the humble wee tree, so diminutive it could fit in the heart, you see. From it hung seven revered ornaments of inestimable worth, handpicked by God, and placed there, not willy-nilly, but with purpose and design. Squint, if you must, to see the wee tree. At first it may look blurry, but perhaps if you close your eyes and open your heart, then you will see.

Evincing a lustrous sheen when caught by the light, a satin heart, bejeweled with glittering diamonds and edged with fine-tatted Irish lace, graced the top of the tree. It honored a mother, and the heights to which her heart soared, after falling deeply in love.

Dangling precariously from the base of the heart's lace, the silhouette of a gentleman's face, profiled a father's life. Its details were left unseen, except for one – that he held onto love.

Spied on the left side of the tree, a spray of forget-me-nots tied with ribbons and bows, recalled a great cloud of heavenly witnesses who bound on their hearts and left behind mysteries to be unraveled and seen. To the right, swayed a not-so-insignificant wicker basket, spilling over with delectable delights turning gray topsy-turvy days right side up, as Mrs. Rogers breezed by, bringing homemade goodies to prisoners of poverty she had not forgotten.

Rays of radiant light illuminated a crucifix affixed to the center of the tree. Distinguished in size, it safeguarded the humble church there at its side.

Behold the Word Incarnate, hanging on the cross, whose body given up, spoke so eloquently of love. How beautiful the head, crowned with the prickly piercing thorns that laughed at death, which lost its sting. How beautiful the hands that once stretched out to make a leper clean, and now bleeding and soiled, stretched out and were nailed to a tree. How beautiful the feet that brought glad tiding, proclaiming liberty to captives, and now with one spike were hopelessly tethered to the tree. How beautiful the pierced side, inviting all mankind to bathe in the graces and mercies poured out like a purifying deluge from within. To the One who is the center of all seen and unseen, the Lamb who sits on the center of the throne, all without exception, bend the knee.

Look inside the humble church. Do you see the living stones built from the side of Christ, the chief cornerstone? Gathered together, with their friend Father Grover Bell, at the kingly banquet set before paupers in need, all offer thanksgiving and praise to the One recognized in the breaking of the bread.

Regal in regard, most exquisite of all, the seventh ornament was to enkindle a longing to look beyond to what was unseen. Bend the knee to catch a glimpse, for it hangs underneath, supporting the tree. Visible to those with eyes to see, the pearl of great price, with flashing streams of effulgent light like sunburst bright, spotlighted a wonder-filled gift placed under the tree. Stamped with a mysterious royal insignia, "Beatitude," this treasure, buried in sorrowful dejection but resurrected in joyful bliss, would be opened to them on that day when memories melted away in the burning warmth of ecstasy's first embrace.

Christians know that they are a royal race and are sharers in the office of the priesthood. For what is more king-like than to find yourself ruler over your body after having surrendered your soul to God? And what is more priestly than to promise the Lord a pure conscience and to offer him in love unblemished victims on the altar of one's heart?

Saint Leo the Great

Chapter 8

Masquerading as nobility, sporting a floppy laurel of putrefied shriveled up flesh atop his skeletal head, he rode with an air of bravado, the marauder, diabolical death. Into the darkness of night, in a frenzy to outdistance heaven's light, his stealthy steed devoured the ground, ravenous for the scent of death at the bedside of the departing dead. Cackling a sinister cry at their demise, scooping up his prey, off he dashed through the valley of death, heedless to the wails and sobs of suffering left. With maniacal delight and insatiable passion, spraying his fetid fumes like puffs of false vainglory in the night air, down, down, down he flew to dispatch his spoils into the pit of the never-ending death. No respecter of life, incredulous was he to their flickering light of love, the breath of God within.

In a flash, before the One on the white horse who rode the clouds, death and horse lay stunned. This one, the Lord of lords and King of kings, called faithful and true, demanded back these two caught in the throes of death. Partakers and feasters on the bread of life, never would they be subject to the abysmal inferno of the lake of fire known as the second unending death. No, victors were they over death. Victors were they with their names written in the book of life. Victors were they to receive the crown of life.

In the year King Uzziah died, Isaiah saw the Lord. When death spirited away Johnny and Mame, the parents Mary loved, when fire burned away the straw and hay of their lives, what was it that Mary saw?

After the deaths of Dorothy and Jackie, when the

stars lost their luster and the zest for life ebbed away, to whom did they go seeking consolation after suffering's embrace? Carrying their unrelenting sorrows, to the plains they went, hoping beyond hope to hear a consoling refrain. Attentive to His words, they heard, "Blessed are they who mourn for they will be comforted." Imploring help in abating their distress, to the foot of the cross they went. Who was there at the foot of the cross? Who collected every tear flowing from their woeful eyes? Who refashioned them into precious jewels, placing them in their children's heavenly crowns?

Another mother was there, a mother who understood, for she also walked along a sorrowful road, the Via Dolorosa with her son. It was there at the foot of the cross where these two souls, familiar with desolation so great, left their offering of resignation at the altar of grace.

Through all her parent's tribulations, was God ever put on trial, found wanting and left to die in their souls? Scrutinize their lives. To whom did they witness if not to Him? Were their hands not like His – outstretched to give rather than outstretched to receive? Were their feet not like His – quick to walk the extra mile to support family members in need? Were their ears not attentive to His word, putting it into practice with their many loving deeds? Were their eyes not stayed on Him even in their unilluminated dismal days? Like St. Anselm, had their hearts not found what they were looking for? And were they not burning with love's fire upon finding Him within?

For they approached, not Mt. Sinai with its fiery smoke and fearsome trumpet blasts, but they approached Mt. Zion and were touched by Him. His touch was more excellent than the touch of Elisha's bones upon a dead man, bringing him back to life. It was more cleansing than the River Jordan upon Naaman's leprous skin. It was more powerful than the embers upon Isaiah's lips, purging the wickedness within.

Penetrating through sinews and the marrow imprisoned in the bones, His touch was able to transform and satiate the inner sanctum of the soul with its bountiful, soothing balm, the sublimity of the divine, moving it to cry out like the apostle Thomas, "my Lord and my God."

It was to this One with the intimate touch, the cornerstone who was able to unite body and soul to the divine, to whom Johnny and Mame came and with hearts bowed before Him, hailed Him as king.

Yes, all that Mary saw when examining her parents' lives well, she understood. For when He lured her into the desert, He not only spoke to her heart, but with one touch, He captured hers as well.

Lord, my heart is not proud; nor are my eyes haughty. I do not busy myself with great matters, with things too sublime for me. Rather, I have stilled my soul, hushed it like a weaned child, like a weaned child on its mother's lap, so is my soul within me.

Psalm 131:1-2

Chapter 9

Oh, where have you flown, you by-gone days, heaped so high like the sands of time? Blown away were you, like a vanishing mist into the sunsets of yesterday, and twilight fast approaches, settling in with a new stillness of life at this hour of eventide.

Youth's rosy blush upon the cheeks now faded to furrowed lines upon the sallow face. Agile fingers that once tacked the frilly frock, now gnarled and stiff, feigned at stitching the ruffled dress. Fast-paced high heels that once clipped along stepped down to tennis shoes that faltered along. Mary, the mother who once carried each child, now, in turn, was carried by them.

Hush yourself, Mary, like a weaned child on its mother's lap. Trust in me, in trust is your strength as you await the final Passover to your new resting place.

Even though old and gray, remembered will you be by me. I have loved you with an age-old love. See upon the palm of my hand, I have written your name. Do not fear or be dismayed. I will not leave you orphaned but will be with you until time's end, recording your good deeds to accompany you then.

From on high, I saw you reconnoiter a new promised land overflowing with life-giving water and gifts of finest wheat. I saw you slay the daunting Anakim giants for your children's sake. I saw your soul joyfully draw water from the fountain of salvation and nourish itself on the supernatural bread. I saw the outside world look at you but strain to see only poverty. Yet, when I looked, I saw within a heart, like a crucible of Ophir's finest gold, receiving and pumping out the sacrificial royal blood of the daughter of the king.

Do not be afraid. Be courageous. Be stouthearted. Persevere. Seek your delight in me. I will return for you, my faithful one. Wait for me. When all seems painted in a patina of liquid gold, when angelic choirs seem but an earshot away, I will be there. Come to me.

Happy the man watching daily at my gate, waiting at my doorposts. For he who finds me, finds life and wins favor from the Lord.

Proverbs 8:14

Chapter 10

World, oh world, that tugged on the senses so long, whose very cares choked the life of the soul within, withered, shriveled up are you like a parched arid wasteland with nothing left to give.

As interest in outward trappings acquiesced to inner sensibilities, a body constrained loosed a soul which took to flight, soaring to loftier heights. Beyond previous imaginings, a higher realm exuding an exhilarating air intoxicating in its allure, insinuated itself upon Mary's soul. Sublime and pristine, bordering on the mystical, never before had such a wondrous vision been seen.

Bathed in amber's soft glow, but with the added dimension as if viewing it through the glimmering translucency of a golden topaz stone, it was as though all around summoned the sun to shed its light on this dipped-in-honey dazzling site. Even the city of God could not hold bound the light and sounds that drifted to this sacred place that quickened the heart and soul of those who passed through this sun-drenched courtyard outside of heaven's gate.

It was here, in the unearthly gleam of electrum radiating off the gilded filigree upon the burnished gates, that Mary danced and sang her canticle of praise. Serendipitous moments of winsome days burst forth, as effortlessly she twirled and spun to the sweet melodious distant sounds of timbrel and lyre carried about in the celestial air. Her flowing, gold-threaded sequined gown with pearls set in gold, swished and swayed, resembling the dance of the sun on the glistening dew atop a brightly bejeweled meadow of buttery buttercups.

Amid trumpet blasts and shouts of joy, joining the heavenly host, could be heard her thanksgiving and praise to the kinsmen redeemer who gave His life as a ransom price to buy her back from death, to the bread from heaven who once walked the Earth and here remained, giving her a share in the heavenly banquet again and again, to the One clothed with radiant light, who set his foot and left his light as he passed through the courtyard and caught her eye.

Lovingly He looked upon Mary, a mere breath, a mere shadow of her former self, the beggar with a heart of gold who waited for Him outside the gate. Soon, yes very soon, He would come and carry her home to plant her in the courts on the other side of the gate.

To fall in love with God is the greatest romance, to seek Him the greatest adventure, to find Him, the greatest heavenly achievement.

— Saint Augustine

Chapter 11

Mother Mary, so fragile, so frail, your body, pierced and poured out, mirrors the legend of the pelican who gave her blood to nourish her perishing young. Your eyes, riveted with an unwavering gaze, reveal the story of a longing soul, discerning someone so close, yet obscure as if veiled and so far away. Who has ravished your heart with their irresistible magnetism and claimed it as their own?

Look deeply into her eyes. Linger awhile and you will see the One for whom her heart pines. But mindful of God's unsullied holiness, heedfully ready yourself as He lifts the veil to reveal the breathtaking loveliness of His sweet, longing face.

Mother Mary, did you know that every stitch in your little girls' dresses was a stitch in your new wedding dress and that every loving act was a jewel in your new crown of life? Did you know that every grueling long hour worked to provide your family a roomier house was building you a heavenly home? Did you know that all the Masses and rosaries sent on ahead, not to curry favor like Jacob with Esau, but simply to say, "My heart belongs to You alone," was binding yours to His in an inseparable way? Had you any idea that when you reached for the stars within your grasp was the bright morning star?

Close your eyes, mother Mary. Night comes, darkness descends and man's work is done. It is the close of day. Father Robert Hermann has anointed you for the journey to your new home, now, but a breath away. All your years of "yes" to that familiar, loving voice, comes down to this one final "yes," a glorious one.

Know that all your eyes looked upon will not be closed to you, but brought to fullness at the break of the new dawn which scatters the darkness and welcomes the true light of the perfect day. Approach the transcendent without trepidation, you soul that loved the Lord. Contemplate the incomparable at the opening of the gate.

A state of ambivalence as if suspended between two different worlds, one familiar and the other unknown, tested and vexed her soul. Out of the depths, she cried: "Come, Lord Jesus! Pray me home, mother and father. Pray me home you holy souls and saints of old. With your safety ring me around, good Saint Joseph and all you angelic host."

Spellbinding melodious strains of angelic lauds assuaged the anguish within. Their sweet-sounding chant of praise magnified with each resounding rhapsodic refrain, until choruses of alleluias reached a crescendo – one glorious exaltation, heralding the arrival of the King of kings.

A footfall, the rustling of a robe, an aromatic bouquet of myrrh, aloes and cassia filling the expectant air, a whisper of undying love, a breathtaking kiss, a warm caress placating the throes of death, and a body reposed loosed a captive soul.

At the sound of the trumpet's blast and clarion call, "Open wide, you victory gate," the King spoke, saying, "Rise up in splendor my beloved, my beautiful one. Mary, my daughter, in whom I delight. Come to me."

*Listen my daughter,
and understand;
pay me careful heed.
Forget your people
and your Father's
house. That the king
might desire your
beauty. He is your
Lord; honor him
daughter... All
glorious is the King's
daughter as she
enters, her raiment
threaded with gold.*

Psalm 45:11-14

Chapter 12

Let all who enter through the gate into the courts of the living city, regaled in the resplendent light, enter rejoicing, giving thanks, singing hymns of praise and blessing God's holy name. For even the stones in the city's walls shine forth extolling His majesty.

Pulsating, as if vivified with life, jasper, chalcedony, topaz and gems of beryl, scatter their rays of brilliant light, with carefree abandonment, adorning His holy face. Amethyst and sapphire robe Him in shades of violet and purplish blue, befitting His majesty. Hyacinth, emerald and sardonyx, gather together with carnelian, chrysolite and chrysoprase, to drizzle down their multifaceted light like shimmering stars strewn at his feet. Why, even the sacred incense, permeating the heavens with its bounteous blend of storax, onycha, galbanum and pure frankincense, rises like billowy puffs of glimmering gold reflecting off the altar below. But vying for the crowning honor of embellishing heaven's masterpiece, light as though dispersed through a prism, configures a rainbow encircling His royal throne.

Has any eye, which feasted on the world's splendor, come near to envisioning the unsurpassed glory of God declared in the heavens? Has any sweet sound that pleased the ear come near to the transporting ecstasy of the soothing seraphic rhapsodies? Has any soul, that savored whispers of undying love overheard in the stillness of night, come near to fathoming its immeasurable magnitude? Has any mind conceived of what God has prepared for those who love Him?

Oh, cover yourselves, you rapturous sights that sear

themselves upon the soul with their unforeseen intimate delights. Still yourselves, you angelic hosts, for there is only so much joy a soul can hold. But cover themselves they could not for they were not the source of the bedazzling light. Nor, still themselves could they, for love's passionate expression is set ablaze with the vision of the divine face to face.

Draw near to the throne of mercy, you unencumbered soul as transparent as byssus silk. Survey the inheritance bequeathed to you borne on my pledge of love. Be attentive to the four living creatures, unceasingly exclaiming: "Holy, holy, holy is the Lord God almighty, who was, and who is and who is to come." Witness the twenty-four elders falling down in worship, tossing their golden crowns before the throne.

Come to the bridal chamber, Mary. Your bridegroom awaits. Step into the wedding-day canvas painted for you. Drink freely and deeply from love's inexhaustible wedding cup. Enter into the all-consuming union of bliss where two hearts, in love, forever beat as one.

> For the wedding day of the Lamb has come; his bride has made herself ready.
>
> Revelation 19:2